For everyone with a little heart. ❤

To my joyful mother, "Ma".
For always encouraging me to
"Choose Happy."

H is for Happy: An Emoji ABC Book of Feelings

First Edition

Good Human Books
Chicago, IL

Emojis provided by EmojiOne

For special discounts, bulk purchases,
press inquiries or educational needs:
Sales@GoodHumanBooks.com

Message the author:
Evan@GoodHumanBooks.com

For additional information and resources visit:
www.HisforHappy.com

For more "Picture Books With a Purpose" visit:
www.GoodHumanBooks.com

Follow the journey:
@GoodHumanBooks

Made in the USA
Additional printing information
may be found on the last page.

ISBN-13: 978-0-692-93645-0
ISBN-10: 0692936459

H is for HAPPY

An Emoji ABC Book of Feelings

By Evan Nimke

THIS HAPPY BOOK BELONGS TO:

____

How do you feel?

Feelings range from A to Z

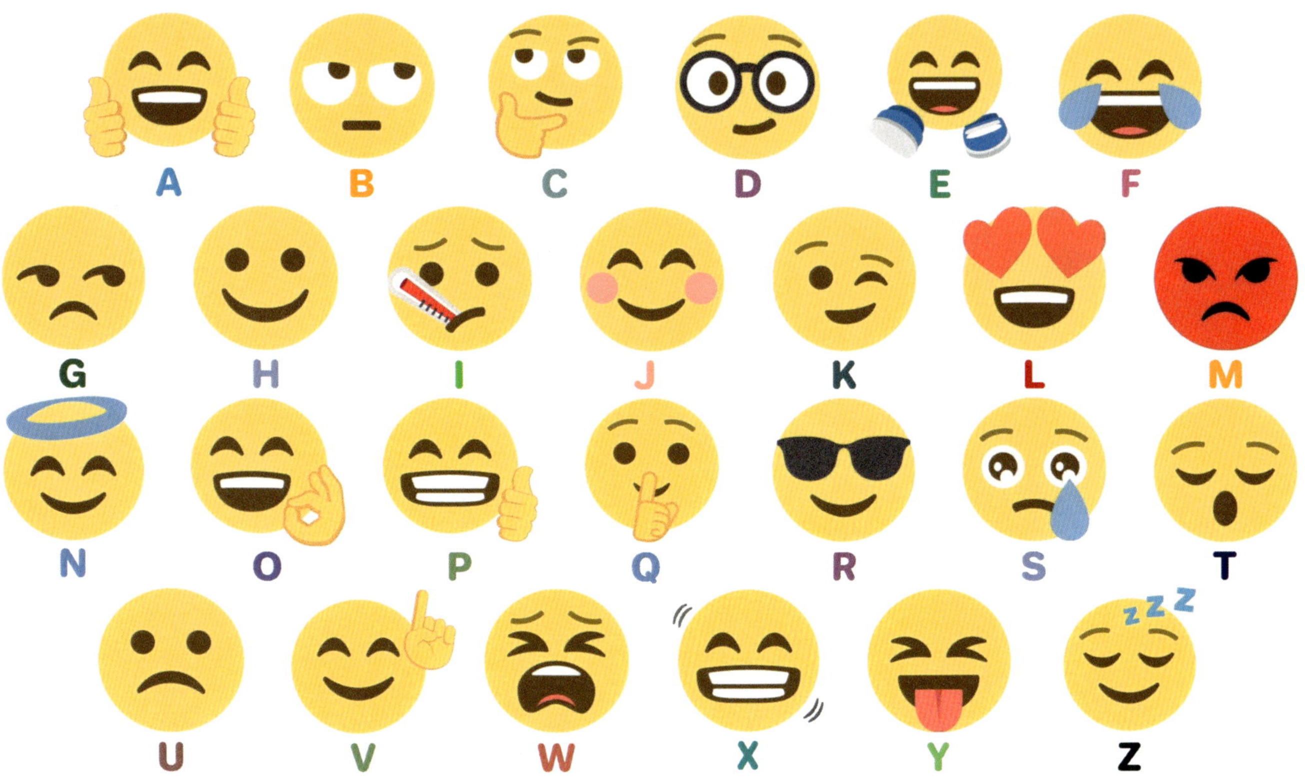

Naming these feelings is as easy as A-B-C ...

A is for AWESOME

The way I feel when I'm with you!

B is for BORED

Time to think of something new.

C is for CURIOUS

Thinking and wondering.

D is for DIFFERENT

We're all unique; it's a beautiful thing!

E is for ENERGETIC

Ready to play play play!

F is for FUNNY

HA HA HA! What made you laugh today?

G is for GRUMPY

If you're grumpy - I suggest more rest!

H is for HAPPY

You make me happy - your smile is the best!

I is for ILL

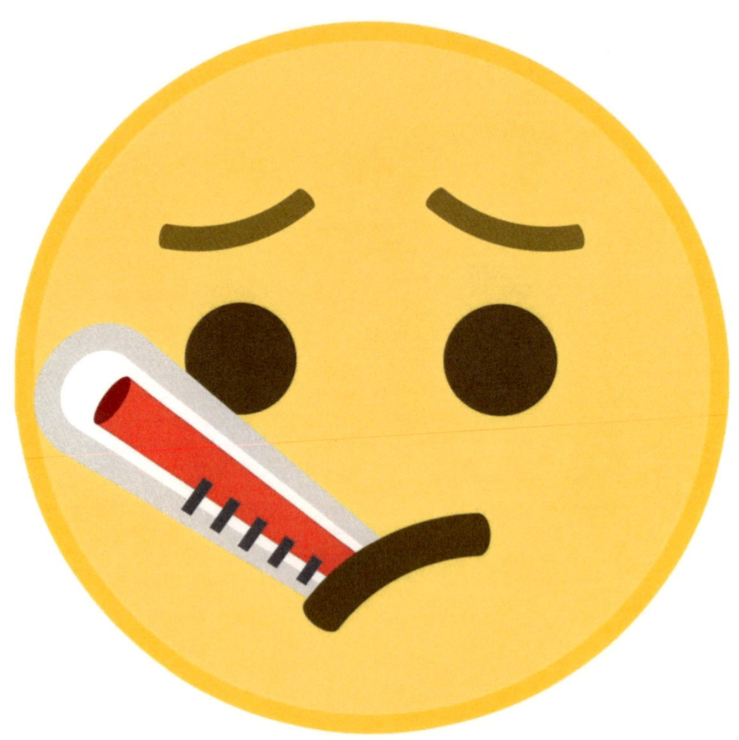

Sick and icky head to toes.

J is for JOYFUL

When your happiness overflows!

K is for KIND

Sharing and caring every day.

L is for LOVE

Hugs and kisses make my heart feel this way.

M is for MAD

Don’t throw a fit - take a deep breath or two.

N is for NICE

Saying "*sorry,*" "*please,*" and "*thank you.*"

O is for OPTIMISTIC

Don’t worry - everything is A-OK!

P is for PROUD

You make me proud every single day!

Q is for QUIET

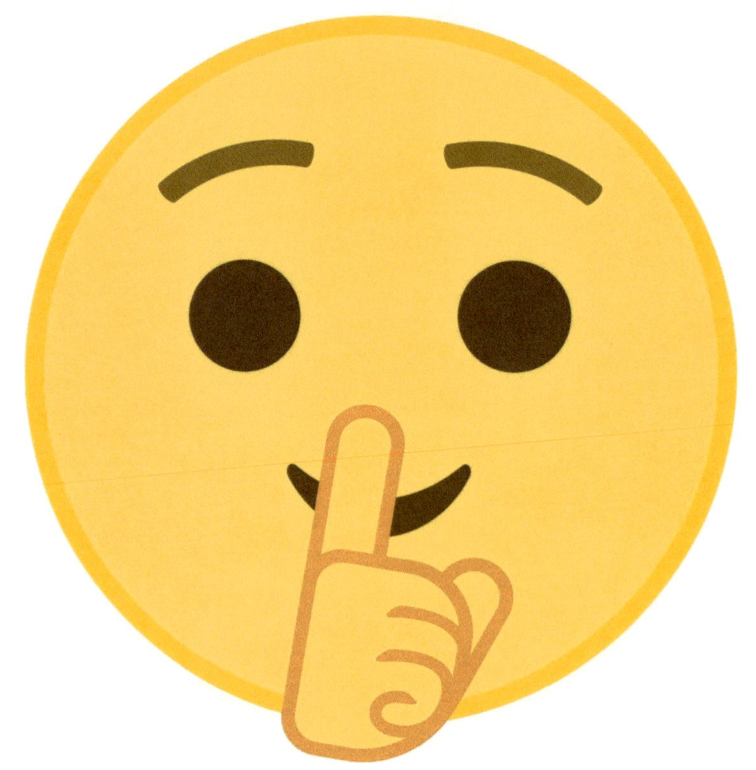

Shhh "inside voices" please.

R is for RELAXED

Calm and comfy - feeling at ease.

S is for SAD

We all get sad sometimes and that's OK!

T is for TIRED

Mommies and Daddies often feel this way.

U is for UPSET

A *frowny* feeling that isn't much fun.

V is for VICTORIOUS

Winning a challenge - feeling like #1!

W is for WHINY

Please don't *whine* if you have something to say.

X is for EXCITED

For a big surprise or super special day!

Y is for YUCKY

A disgusting feeling I do not like!

ZZz is for SLEEPY

Tuck me in tight and turn off the light!

Feelings range from A to Z

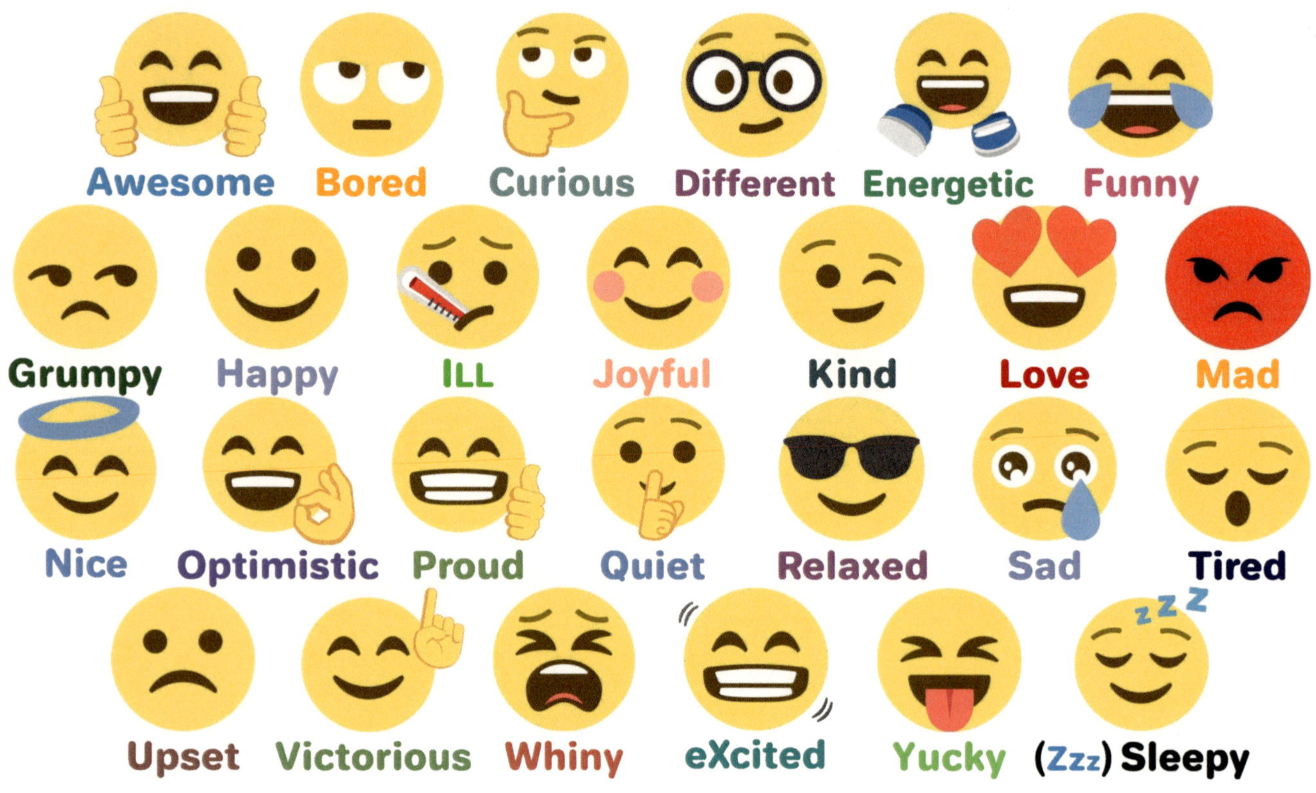

Now naming your feelings is as easy as A-B-C!

And always remember...

EVERYONE

WHAT MADE YOU FEEL HAPPY TODAY?

"H" IS FOR HAPPY "S" IS FOR SAD SOMETIMES YOU FEEL GOOD SOMETIMES YOU FEEL BAD FEELINGS RANGE FROM A-TO-Z THEY CAN MAKE YOUR DAY OR DRIVE YOU CRAZY SOME MAKE YOU FEEL BIG SOME MAKE YOU FEEL SMALL IN JUST ONE DAY YOU MIGHT FEEL THEM ALL EVERYTHING YOU FEEL IS OK AS LONG AS YOU FEEL IT IN A GOOD AND POSITIVE WAY EVERYONE HAS FEELINGS AND DESERVES TO BE HAPPY WHEN YOU CARE ABOUT SOMEONE ELSE'S FEELINGS THAT'S CALLED EMPATHY EMPATHY IS AWESOME IT'S NEVER TOO LATE TO START ...ALL IT TAKES IS A LITTLE HEART.❤

THE 🙂 END

T is for Thank You.

To my wife Jenn
for always supporting me and never laughing at my crazy ideas.

To my friends, family and their children
for proofing the early drafts and being my tiny editorial board.

To my little humans, Grayson and Brayden
for your inspiration. You are my greatest adventure - you are my "happy thought."

ABOUT THE AUTHOR
THE STORY BEHIND THE STORY

I was inspired to write this book by my own experiences as a stay-at-home dad trying to teach my kids about feelings and empathy. Throughout that time I was fortunate to have front row seats to the daily emotional fireworks show put on by my two boys as I watched them explore - and explode, trying to understand their newfound emotions. I witnessed firsthand how challenging it can be for children to express their feelings without knowing the words to describe them.

Unable to find any ABC books about feelings at home or the library, I set out during my kid's naptime to create one myself and titled it *H is for Happy*.

Intrigued by my son's fascination with emojis on my phone - I wondered if those same little yellow faces could help them identify and name their own emotions. I matched up letters of the alphabet with a corresponding emoji and gave it a shot! I wanted to teach them the names of their feelings, but more importantly, let them know everything they feel is okay and that they are not alone – everyone has feelings!

To my amazement after just a few reads, my oldest began identifying and saying "Happy," "Tired," "Sad," and even "Daddy Proud." When he gave his most coveted Buzz Lightyear hoodie to his crying baby brother to make him "feel better," that's when I realized this might be more than just a little homemade ABC book.

I'll never forget that "feel better" moment or hearing them say "happy" for the first time - it's the reason I decided to publish this book and my motivation to share it with as many parents and children as possible. I hope it has as positive an impact on you and your child's life as it has on mine - or, if nothing else, allows you to end your "beautifully chaotic" days as a parent with a happy thought and a smile from your child.

A happy today starts with you. A happier tomorrow starts with our children.

Choose Happy.

DO MORE
OF WHAT
MAKES YOU
HAPPY

www.HisforHAPPY.com

48760753R00027

Made in the USA
Columbia, SC
11 January 2019